GERMANY

Ting Morris and Rachel Wright

W
FRANKLIN WATTS

This symbol appears on some
pages throughout this book. It
indicates that adult supervision
is advisable for that activity.

This edition 2007

Franklin Watts
338 Euston Road
London NW1 3BH

Franklin Watts Australia
Hachette Children's Books
Level 17/207 Kent Street
Sydney, NSW 2000

© Franklin Watts 1993, 2003

Editor: Hazel Poole
Designer: Sally Boothroyd
Commissioned photography: Peter Millard
Artwork: Teri Gower
Picture research: Ambreen Husain, Annabel Martin, Juliet Duff

A CIP catalogue record for this book is available
from the British Library.

ISBN-13 978 0 7496 7336 9

Printed in China

Franklin Watts is a division of Hachette Children's Books.

CONTENTS

Introducing Germany

WILLKOMMEN IN DEUTSCHLAND!

Germany lies in northern Central Europe and covers an area of 357,000 square kilometres. Between 1949 and 1990, Germany was divided into two different countries - West Germany and East Germany. They were reunited in 1990. Germany has borders with Poland, the Czech Republic, Austria, Switzerland, France, Luxembourg, Belguim, the Netherlands and Denmark.

The German flag has three stripes - black, red and gold. These were the colours of the Weimar Republic. The national coat of arms shows an eagle, a symbol originally brought to Germany by the Romans.

CAPITAL CITY

The capital city of Germany is Berlin. It is Germany's largest city. Bonn was the capital city until 1991. It was also the seat of government. In 1999 the government moved to the *Reichstag* in Berlin.

NATIONAL ANTHEM

The national anthem is the third verse of the *Deutschlandlied* (Song of Germany). The music was composed by Joseph Haydn in 1797, and the words were written by Hoffmann von Fallersleben in 1841. The song became the German national anthem in 1922.

MONEY AND STAMPS

The unit of currency in Germany is the *euro*. It replaced the *Deutsche Mark* in February 2002. One euro is divided into 100 *cents*. Bank notes are available in: 5, 10, 20, 50, 100, 200 and 500 euros, and coins in 1 and 2 euros, as well as 1, 2, 5, 10, 20 and 50 cents.

The *Deutsche Bundespost* is the German Federal Post Office, which issues all German stamps.

CAR REGISTRATION

In Germany you drive on the right-hand side of the road, so the steering wheel is on the left. By looking at the registration number, you can tell which part of Germany a car comes from. The first letters tell you where the car is registered, for example F stands for Frankfurt.

GOVERNMENT

Germany is a federal republic - its German name is the *Bundesrepublik Deutschland*. The Federal President is head of state, but it is the Chancellor who is the head of the government. Parliament is made up of two houses - the *Bundestag*, which is the most powerful, and the *Bundesrat*.

> **Say it in German:**
> *die Briefmarke* - stamp
> *das Auto* - car
> *die Fahne* - flag
> *das Geld* - money
> *die Großstadt* - city
> *das Postamt* - post office

Around Germany

Germany is made up of 16 individual states *(Länder)*. The largest is Bavaria and the smallest is Bremen. Each state has its own capital and regional government. Look at the map to see where the different states are.

GERMAN GEOGRAPHY

The northern part of Germany is made up of a flat, fertile plain and this area is heavily farmed. In central Germany, deep river valleys and gorges run through rocky and forested hills. Here you can find the Harz Mountains.

In southern Germany, there are more hills and higher mountains. The land between the hills makes good farmland. The Bavarian Alps in the south-east contain Germany's highest mountain, the *Zugspitze*, which is 2,963 metres high.

THE BLACK FOREST

The Black Forest *(Schwarzwald [below])*, in the south-west, is a mountainous area named after the thick forests of dark fir trees that cover the slopes. It is a famous setting for many German legends and folk tales.

CASTLE NEUSCHWANSTEIN

This 19th century fairytale castle *(centre)* was built for King Ludwig II of Bavaria. Walt Disney used it as the model for Sleeping Beauty's castle.

COLOGNE (KÖLN)

Cologne, on the River Rhine, was founded by the Romans. It is a busy city and is an important commercial centre. It is popular with visitors who come to see its famous cathedral *(above)*.

CLIMATE

Germany has a mild climate. Winter fogs and cloudy days are common in the north. Further south, the summers are warmer and the winters colder. South of the central highlands, mountain peaks are usually snowcapped all winter. There is moderate rainfall throughout the country in all seasons.

Average temperatures		
Place	January	July
Hamburg	0°C	17°C
Cologne	2°C	18°C
Munich	-1°C	18°C

HAMELN (HAMELIN)

This town is famous for the story of the Pied Piper. According to legend, the town was plagued by rats and was saved by a mysterious piper. He led the rats away from the town but was refused payment for his help. As a result, he led the town's children away - never to be seen again.

BRANDENBURG GATE

The Brandenburg Gate *(left)* is one of Berlin's most famous sights. Built between 1788 and 1791, it overlooks the remains of the wall that divided the city for 28 years.

NATIONAL COSTUME

Today, regional costumes are often only worn for festivals and on special occasions. In Bavaria, however, some people still wear traditional costume everyday. Women wear the *Dirndl*, a dress with a full gathered skirt and a fitted bodice. Men wear *Lederhosen* (leather shorts), especially when rambling.

DIALECTS

Standard, or High, German (*Hochdeutsch*) is the official form of the German language. However, many people still speak with a hint of their native district's dialect. This is particularly true in the south where the Bavarian dialect is used. Traces of Low German (*Plattdeutsch*) are found in northern Germany. This dialect is still spoken in the countryside near the seacoast.

Say it in German
der Fluß - river
der Berg - mountain
der Baum - tree
das Schloß - castle
der Sommer - summer
der Winter - winter
der Regen - rain

Food and Drink

Germans are known for enjoying good, plain food. Many German recipes were created hundreds of years ago to stop food from spoiling. *Sauerkraut* (pickled cabbage) and *Sauerbraten* (marinated beef) are examples of this. Meat was also preserved by making sausages such as *Bratwurst*. Germany is still the home of the sausage and each region has its own special recipe for sausages.

German beers and wines are famous all over the world for their high quality. Lager is more popular in Germany than any other country. You can find breweries in almost every town.

REGIONAL FOOD

The German climate is good for growing crops and farms produce a lot of the country's food. The main crops are cabbages, potatoes, wheat, rye, sugar beet and grapes.

For breakfast, people usually have bread rolls (*Brötchen*) with jam or sausage, and coffee. Lunch is very often the main meal of the day and will usually consist of a meat dish, perhaps pork. In the afternoon, especially on a Sunday, many people enjoy a cup of coffee and a piece of cake (*Kaffee und Kuchen*). Dinner is often a light meal of bread, cheese and sausage.

Each region has its own specialities. Here are just a few:

MENU

Weißwurst - veal sausage (Bavaria)

Schwarzwälder Kirschtorte - Black Forest cherry cake (Black Forest)

Pfefferpothast - goulash with pepper (Westphalia)

Aalsuppe - eel soup (Hamburg area)

Thüringer Sauerbraten mit Klößen - braised beef with dumplings (Saxony and Thuringia)

Himmel und Erde - puréed potato and apple with fried sausage (Rhineland).

Say it in German
der Bauernhof - farm
das Frühstück - breakfast
das Mittagessen - lunch
das Abendessen - dinner

A Taste of Germany

Potato dishes are popular in Germany, particularly *Kartoffelpuffer* (potato cakes), which are often served with apple sauce.

YOU WILL NEED:

1 teaspoon water
dish
large mixing bowl
thick bottomed frying pan
cooking oil
tablespoon
sharp knife
fork
500g cooking apples
1 large egg
1 onion
1 teaspoon lemon juice
3 level tablespoons plain flour
salt and pepper
saucepan with lid
grater
1 kg potatoes
fish slice
potato peeler

To make the apple sauce

1. Peel the apples and cut them into quarters. Carefully remove the core and slice each quarter thinly.

2. Put the apples, lemon juice and water into the saucepan and bring the mixture to the boil over a medium heat.

3. Turn down the heat so that the mixture bubbles only slightly. Cover with the lid and leave the apples to cook for 10 -15 minutes until soft.

4. Turn off the heat and spoon the apple sauce into the dish.

To make the potato cakes

5. Wash and peel the potatoes. Grate them, and the onion, into the bowl. Mind your fingers!

6. Add the egg, flour, half a teaspoon of salt and a sprinkling of pepper to the potato mixture and mix everything together.

7. Heat some oil in the frying pan over a low heat. The oil should completely cover the bottom of the pan.

8. Drop 3 tablespoonfuls of the potato mixture into the pan. Shape the mixture into a round cake, about 1 cm thick, with the fish-slice.

9. Fry the cakes for three minutes on each side until they are crisp and golden brown.

10. When your cakes are ready, serve them immediately with the apple sauce.

Shopping

German people like to buy fresh food every day, and fruit and vegetables are often sold in street markets. Many of the smaller grocer's shops are being replaced by supermarkets and every town also has a hypermarket.

Shops are normally open from 9 am to 6.30 pm on weekdays, and until 2 pm on Saturdays. On the first Saturday in the month, shops stay open all day. This is called a *langer Samstag* (long Saturday).

In larger towns, many department stores and other shops can be found in special pedestrian precincts. These are areas where no cars are allowed. Germany was one of the first countries to provide these precincts.

Die Konditorei sells cakes, pastries, chocolates and biscuits. You can also sit down to enjoy a cup of coffee with your cake.

Die Bäckerei opens at 7 am in time to sell fresh rolls for breakfast and other types of bread. The bread is normally baked on the premises.

Die Metzgerei sells raw meat, as well as a variety of sausages and other cooked meats.

Shopping List

das Brot - bread
die Milch - milk
das Obst - fruit
das Gemüse - vegetables
der Zucker - sugar
der Fisch - fish
der Käse - cheese
der Kaffee - coffee
die Wurst - sausage
die Kartoffel - potato

Say it in German

der Laden - shop
das Lebensmittelgeschäft - grocer
der Supermarkt - supermarket
der Großmarkt - hypermarket
die Fußgängerzone - pedestrian precinct

FIND YOUR WAY! You are enjoying a cup of coffee with a friend at your local *Konditorei* when you suddenly discover that you've both left your wallets in different shops. Using your finger, retrace your route back to *die Bäckerei* and *die Metzgerei*, then hurry back to *die Konditorei* before the waitress notices that you've gone.

German Life

WHERE PEOPLE LIVE

More than 80 per cent of German people live in towns and cities. Many live in small apartments in modern blocks. Housing is very expensive, so most people rent their apartments. Gardens are usually small and some people rent an allotment where they can grow flowers and have a small summer house.

In the picturesque villages in rural Germany, people lead a more traditional way of life. In the Alpine villages in the south of Germany, you can see chalet-style housing.

Housing in Germany varies from the village alpine houses in the south to apartments found in cities.

SCHOOL

School starts at 8 am, so children often leave home in the dark in winter. Most schools end between 12 noon and 1 pm, and children go home for lunch. German children have quite a lot of homework, but if they get it done in the afternoon, they then have the evening free.

STUNDENPLAN

Name: Ute Müller Schule: Geschwister-Scholl Realschule Klasse: 5A

Zeit	Montag	Dienstag	Mittwoch	Donnerstag	Freitag	Samstag
8.00-8.45	Deutsch	Werken	Mathe	Englisch	Religion	Sport
8.50-9.35	Deutsch	Mathe	Biologie	Englisch	Deutsch	Sport
9.40-10.25	Turnen	Englisch	Deutsch	Biologie	Geschichte	Chor
10.30-10.45	Pause	/	/	/	/	/
10.50-11.35	Erdkunde	Kunst	Physik	Werken	Mathe	
11.40-12.25	Religion	Kunst	Musik	Mathe	Physik	
12.30-1.15		Geschichte	Erdkunde		Sozialkunde	

Parents give new pupils a large cone made of cardboard and fancy paper, filled with sweets, on the first day of primary school at the age of six. At the age of 10, children move on to different secondary schools. Students who want to go on to university have to pass an exam to get into a grammar school (*Gymnasium*). After nine years at the *Gymnasium*, students take an exam called the *Abitur*.

Many children cycle to school, and in many places there are special cycle paths where cars and pedestrians are not allowed. They usually run between the road and pavement and have their own traffic lights. This makes cycling safe and convenient, especially in large towns.

WHAT PEOPLE DO

Some people work as farmers either growing crops such as potatoes and cereals, or rearing dairy cows and pigs. There are factories throughout Germany and many people have jobs in industry. The forests and sawmills also employ many people, and in the Alps a lot of people work in the hotels and sports centres.

NEWSPAPERS AND MAGAZINES

German people read more than 26 million newspapers every day. There are 355 daily newspapers and 35 that are published at least twice a week. The most important daily newspapers are the *Frankfurter Allgemeine Zeitung* (published in Frankfurt), the *Süddeutsche Zeitung* (Munich) and the *Berliner Zeitung* (Berlin). The biggest selling newspaper is *Bild Zeitung*, which sells over 4 million copies and is published in 15 different towns.

There are over 9,000 German magazines in total. Among the best sellers are the weekly illlustrated news magazines *Der Spiegel* and *Stern*, and the television periodical *Hör zu*. Comics are also very popular.

Say it in German
das Haus - house
die Wohnung - flat/apartment
der Garten - garden
die Schule - school
das Fahrrad - bicycle
die Zeitung - newspaper
die Zeitschrift - magazine
die Fabrik - factory
der Bauer - farmer
das Sportzentrum - sports centre

Industry and Transport

Germany's industries were practically destroyed during World War II, but they were quickly rebuilt with help from the United States and other countries. Today, about 30 per cent of Germany's workers are employed in industry.

CARS

Germany is the fifth largest producer of cars in the world, selling over 5 million cars in 2001. Famous manufacturers include BMW, Volkswagen, Daimler-Chrysler, Porsche, and Mercedes-Benz. Gottlieb Daimler and Carl Benz built the first cars in 1885. Today, Mercedes-Benz produces luxury cars and commercial vehicles. Volkswagen is the largest German car producer, and the fourth largest in the world. The Volkswagen factory in Wolfsburg is the biggest car plant in Europe. It manufactures the company's most popular model, the "Golf".

PORCELAIN

A small town in Germany, called Meissen, is famous for its porcelain, especially its figurines. You can recognise Meissen porcelain by its symbol of crossed blue swords.

ELECTRICAL GOODS

Germany is also known for its electrical products, with manufacturers such as Bosch, Braun, Miele and Siemens.

ROAD TRANSPORT

Driving is a way of life in Germany, and there are around 50 million cars on the road. Germany was one of the first countries to build a motorway and today there are more than 11,000 kilometres of motorway. There is no fixed speed limit on many parts of the motorways, but there is a recommended speed limit of 130 kilometres per hour.

AIR TRANSPORT

The national airline is Lufthansa. It is based in Frankfurt am Main, which has one of Europe's largest and busiest airports.

LOCAL TRANSPORT

Large cities in Germany have underground railways (*U-Bahn*) as well as the more common trams, suburban railways and bus systems. In cities, fares usually apply to the entire public transport system, so you can change from a tram to a tube, bus or train on the same ticket. You can buy a multiple "strip" ticket (*Mehrfahrtenkarte* or *Streifenkarte*) from a machine (below). These strips are then cancelled in machines at a station, or on a bus or tram.

RAIL

The *Deutsche Bundesbahn* (DB) runs one of the best and fastest rail services in Europe. It has 40,355 kilometres of track connecting all parts of the country. Modern *InterCity Express* (ICE) trains cruise at speeds of up to 330 kilometres per hour, which means that a journey from Hamburg to Munich takes around five hours.

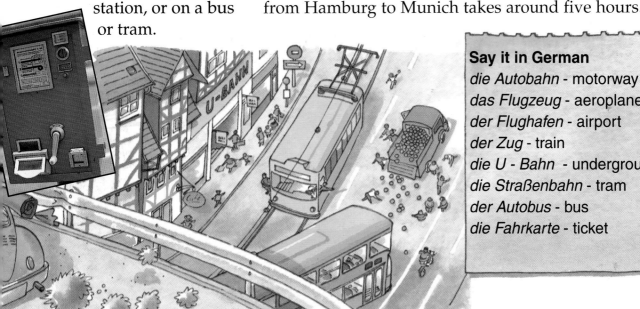

Say it in German
die Autobahn - motorway
das Flugzeug - aeroplane
der Flughafen - airport
der Zug - train
die U - Bahn - underground
die Straßenbahn - tram
der Autobus - bus
die Fahrkarte - ticket

Sport and Leisure

Nearly one in three people belong to a sports club (*Sportverein*) and there are clubs for tennis, swimming, football, shooting and hiking.

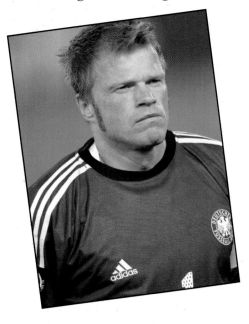

RAMBLING

Many Germans enjoy long country walks. To help ramblers, the best walks are marked with coloured signs on posts and trees. For mountain walkers and climbers, distances are often shown in the length of time it takes to walk to a particular place. In many areas, you will find a *Trimm-dich-Pfad* (keep-fit trail) where you can walk, run and do exercises.

FOOTBALL

Football is Germany's most popular sport. Many top German stars, such as goalkeeper Oliver Kahn (*left*), play club football in the *Bundesliga* (the national league), while others play in countries such as Italy and Spain. Germany's most famous team is Bayern Munich, who play in the Olympic Stadium in Munich.

TENNIS

Tennis is another popular sport and the country has in the past produced top players such as Boris Becker, Steffi Graf and Michael Stich who became national heroes.

SKIING

Many German families go skiing in the Alps in winter. While many go to the neighbouring countries of Austria, Switzerland, France or Italy, Germany itself has some excellent ski resorts. Garmisch-Partenkirchen in the Bavarian Alps is the best known. There are also good resorts in the Black Forest, the Harz region and the Sauerland.

HORSERIDING

Equestrian sports are also very popular. At the top level, German teams are very successful. At the Sydney 2000 Olympics, Germany won gold medals in two team events. Riding schools and clubs can be found throughout Germany, but they can be quite expensive. Cheaper pony treks are available in many parts of the country.

BOAT TRIPS

No visit to the Rhineland is complete without a river trip. Boat trips along the Rhine range from a few hours to days or even a week in length. On a trip between Koblenz and Boppard, you pass 10 castles during the 75-minute voyage! Further upstream, the river narrows near the Lorelei, a 132-metre-high rock. According to legend, a water nymph with golden hair sat on the rock and lured sailors to watery graves with her strange song.

Say it in German:
der Fußball - football
das Tennis - tennis
das Schwimmen - swimming
das Schwimmbad - swimming baths
das Pferd - horse
die Wanderung - ramble

Festivals

Throughout the year, there are many festivals in Germany.

CARNIVAL

In some parts of Germany, the period of time before Lent is known as *Karneval*. In Cologne, for example, everyone dresses up in fancy dress and there is a parade through the town.

In southern Germany, especially Bavaria, carnival is known as *Fasching*. Each town and village has its own carnival prince and princess who lead a costumed procession. As *Fasching* comes to a climax, there are a lot of fancy-dress balls and parties.

CHRISTMAS

Many Christmas customs, including the lighted Christmas tree (*Weihnachtsbaum*) and carols (*Weihnachtslieder*), have a German origin. In Germany, Christmas festivities start early.

Four Sundays before Christmas, the first of the four candles on the Advent garland (*Adventskranz*) is lit.

On 6 December, Saint Nicholas, or Santa Claus, comes to put little presents in children's shoes. He is accompanied by his servant, Ruprecht, who supposedly spanks naughty children with a stick.

Throughout Christmas, special Christmas markets are held in many towns. The largest and most famous of these is in Nuremberg. The highlight is a candle-lit procession, when thousands of children march through the streets.

Presents are opened on Christmas Eve and all the family gathers for the traditional Christmas Day lunch.

THE PASSION PLAY

The pretty village of Oberammergau, in the Bavarian Alps, is best known for its Passion Play, which takes place every 10 years. The play was first performed in 1634, in thanks that the spread of the Plague stopped short of the village. The play shows the final days of Christ and is acted by local villagers. Men grow their hair and beards in the hope of getting a part in the play. The next performance will be in 2010.

OKTOBERFEST

The largest beer festival is the Oktoberfest, held in Munich, and is popular with visitors from all over the world. People dress up in traditional costume.

Say it in German
das Fest - festival
das Weihnachten - Christmas
das Ostern - Easter
das Bier - beer
die Prozession - procession

COUNTDOWN TO CHRISTMAS

Did you know that the first Advent calendar was made in Germany less than 100 years ago?

To make your own Advent calendar

!

YOU WILL NEED:

thin card	tracing paper
pencil	craft knife
metal ruler	cutting board
glue	poster paints
brushes	cardboard

1. Cut the card into two large equal-sized rectangles and paint a nativity scene on one piece and draw 24 little squares onto the other.

2. Then trace the squares onto the illustrated piece of card.

3. Put this piece of card on the cutting board. Using the craft knife, and the metal ruler to guide you, cut along three sides of each square to make windows that open.

4. Paint pictures of Christmas inside the squares on the uncut piece of card. When the paint has dried, glue both pieces of card together, making sure that they are the right way up.

5. Cut out a piece of cardboard the same size as your calendar and glue it onto the back of it. Now number the windows from 1-24, and wait until December 1 when your countdown to Christmas can begin.

Carnival Clowns

YOU WILL NEED:

large plastic bottle
wallpaper paste (fungicide free)
long-sleeved T-shirt
scissors
poster paints
PVA glue
crêpe paper
a pair of big, baggy trouser
newspaper, torn into strips
sandpaper
Stanley knife
face paints
flat elastic
4 safety pins
needle and thread
paint brushes
stiff coloured paper
swimming cap
cardboar
broad ribbon

To make Clumsy Clown Shoes

1. Ask an adult to cut away the top of the plastic bottle and then cut the rest of the bottle in half lengthways.

2. Cut a semi-circle out of the top end of each half of the bottle.

3. Cover the outside of both halves of the bottle with a layer of pasted newspaper. Add another three layers and leave your "shoes" somewhere warm to dry. (This may take quite a while, so it's a good idea to make the other parts of your clown costume while you wait).

4. When your shoes are dry, rub them with sandpaper to make them smooth and then paint them.

5. Ask an adult to pierce two holes at the back of each shoe as shown. Thread a short strip of elastic through each pair of holes and knot the ends.

To wear your clown shoes, slip the elastic under the instep of your ordinary shoes.

To make a Curly Wig

6. Roll strips of coloured paper into curls and glue them onto the swimming cap. *If the cap has a bumpy surface, turn it inside out before you begin.*

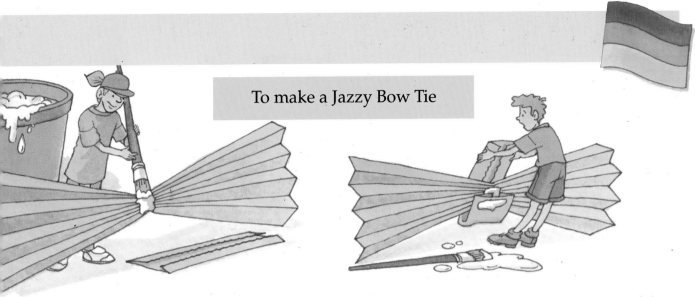

To make a Jazzy Bow Tie

7. Cut out two strips of crêpe paper, one much larger than the other. Fold the smaller strip into thirds. Pleat the larger strip and dab some glue on it as shown.

8. Wrap the folded strip of paper around the middle of the pleated strip and glue it together. Slide a length of elastic, long enough to fit around your neck, through the back of your bow tie and knot the ends.

To make Giant Braces

9. Cut two strips of ribbon, each long enough to reach from the front of your waist, over your shoulder and down to the back of your waist.

10. Turn up the raw edges of both ribbons and sew them into place.

11. Cut out four huge cardboard buttons. Carefully make four holes in each of their centres using the tip of the scissors, and sew them onto the bottom of your braces.

12. Attach your braces to the trousers with safety pins. Make sure that the ribbons cross over at the back.

Now put all your costume together, and get ready to celebrate!

The Arts

Germany has produced many great artists, writers and composers such as Karl Marx, Felix Mendelssohn and Robert Schumann, to name but a few. Here are some others:

ART

Albrecht Dürer (1471-1528)

Dürer was a painter and printmaker famous for his woodcuts (*below*) and engravings. The son of a goldsmith, he became a great scholar and international traveller.

Hans Holbein (1497-1543)
Holbein painted realistic portraits of people. Holbein went to England, painted at the court of Henry VIII (*left*) and had a great influence on English portrait painting.

LITERATURE

The greatest period in German literature was probably between 1750 and 1830.

Johann Wolfgang von Goethe (1749-1832)

Goethe wrote novels, plays and poetry. For most of his life, he worked on his dramatic masterpiece, *Faust*. His early writing influenced the development of German Romanticism.

Friedrich von Schiller (1759 - 1805)

Schiller is most famous for his historical plays. *Don Carlos* is about the Dutch struggle for religious freedom. *Maria Stuart* is about the life and death of Mary Queen of Scots. *Wilhelm Tell* tells the story of the Swiss fight for independence.

Thomas Mann (1875-1955)

Thomas Mann won the Nobel prize for literature in 1929. Eight years later he left Germany, which was then under the control of the Nazis, and went to the United States where he became an American citizen. Mann's novels and short stories deal with the problems of the artist in society.

MUSIC

Johann Sebastian Bach (1685-1750)

Bach composed in every form of music known in his time except opera. Many of his works have been lost, but well over 1,000 have survived. Bach served as *Kantor* (choirmaster and organist) at the Thomaskirche in Leipzig, and the city still holds a Bach festival every four years.

Georg Friedrich Händel (1685-1759)

Händel wrote many operas as well as other great works including *The Messiah* and *Water Music*. He spent most of his adult life in England, where he is known as George Frederick Handel.

Georg Friedrich Händel

Richard Wagner (1813-1883)

Richard Wagner wrote operas based on German legends about giants, knights and magicians. He called these *Musikdramen* (music dramas). His most famous operas are *Lohengrin* and *The Ring of the Nibelung*.

Richard Wagner

Bertolt Brecht

Bertolt Brecht (1898-1956)

Brecht is the most famous German playwright of the 20th century. His most famous work was *The Threepenny Opera*. His plays try to teach as well as entertain.

Ludwig van Beethoven (1770-1827)

Beethoven was one of the world's greatest composers, yet he was almost totally deaf when he died. During his lifetime he composed great music, including nine symphonies. The most famous symphonies are *Eroica* (third), *Pastoral* (sixth) and the ninth.

Ludwig van Beethoven

Say it in German
der Künstler - artist
der Schriftsteller - writer
der Komponist - composer
das Bild - picture
die Musik - music

Fairy Tales and Legends

Germany is a country rich in legend, and its folk tales have become famous all over the world.

Till Eulenspiegel was a German folk hero who lived in the 14th century. He was a mischievous and clever vagabond who roamed the country playing practical jokes on rich and important people. The first book of stories about Till appeared in about 1500. In modern German, a practical joker is still called an *Eulenspiegel*.

The Grimm brothers, Jacob and Wilhelm, were born in Hanau in 1785/6. The first volume of their *Kinder- und Hausmärchen* (Nursery and Household Tales) was published in 1812. Grimms' tales, such as *Hänsel und Gretel*, were very popular because the brothers wrote them down just as they heard them, so that they kept their original spirit.

Baron Münchhausen's full name was Karl Friedrich Hieronymus Freiherr von Münchhausen! He was an 18th century soldier who became famous for the tall stories he told, which were later collected and published. The Baron's incredible travels took him to the moon, through the earth's crust, and over a sea of milk to an island of cheese. He also claimed to have served as a human cannonball in a war against the Turks! Not surprisingly, he is known in German as the *Lügenbaron* ("liar baron") and his adventures are the subject of many books and films.

Max und Moritz was written and illustrated by Wilhelm Busch in 1865 to act as a warning to young children. Max and Moritz are two young children who play tricks on people. They trick the tailor into falling into the river, and he has to be ironed dry. Then they fill the schoolmaster's tobacco-pipe with gunpowder! It is not surprising that the two boys come to a nasty end.

Say it in German
das Märchen - fairy tale
die Legende - legend
die Erzählung - story
das Buch - book
der Film - film

Make a Gingerbread House

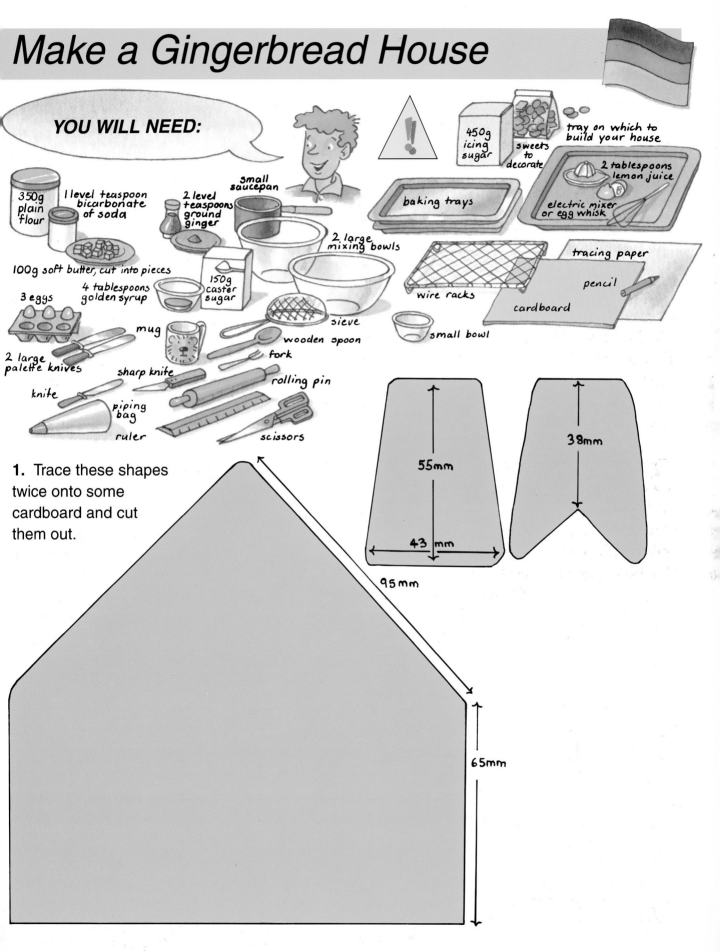

YOU WILL NEED:

350g plain flour

1 level teaspoon bicarbonate of soda

2 level teaspoons ground ginger

100g soft butter, cut into pieces

150g caster sugar

4 tablespoons golden syrup

3 eggs

Small saucepan

2 large mixing bowls

sieve

mug

wooden spoon

fork

2 large palette knives

knife

sharp knife

piping bag

ruler

rolling pin

scissors

450g icing sugar

sweets to decorate

tray on which to build your house

baking trays

2 tablespoons lemon juice

electric mixer or egg whisk

wire racks

small bowl

tracing paper

pencil

cardboard

1. Trace these shapes twice onto some cardboard and cut them out.

55mm

43 mm

95mm

65mm

38mm

To make templates for the side walls and roof

2. Draw two rectangles, 20 cm x 6.5 cm, onto another piece of cardboard and cut them out. Draw some windows and cut them out as well.

3. Draw two rectangles, 23 cm x 11 cm, onto a third piece of cardboard and cut them out. These shapes will form the roof.

To make the gingerbread

4. Sift the flour, bicarbonate of soda and ginger into a mixing bowl.

5. Rub the butter into the flour with your fingertips until the mixture looks like breadcrumbs. Stir in the sugar.

6. Break an egg into the mug and beat it with the fork.

7. Warm the golden syrup in the saucepan over a low heat. *(Grease the tablespoon with butter first to stop the syrup from sticking to it).*

8. Add the syrup and the egg to the flour. Stir with the wooden spoon, then knead with your hands until you have a smooth dough.

9. Pre-heat the oven to 350°F/180°C/gas mark 4.

10. Roll out the dough on a floured surface until it is about 3mm thick. Lay your templates on top of the dough and cut around them using the tip of the sharp knife.

11. Grease the inside of the baking trays, and ask an adult to help you transfer your gingerbread shapes to them using the palette knives. If any of the gingerbread loses its shape, re-roll it and start again.

12. Bake your shapes in the centre of the oven for 10 -15 minutes. Then put them on the wire racks to cool.

To make the icing

13. Crack an egg in half and separate the yolk from the white. Don't allow any yolk to mix with the white. Repeat with another egg.

14. Whisk the egg whites until they are frothy. Sift the icing sugar into a small bowl, then add it to the egg whites a spoonful at a time. Make sure that you beat the mixture well after each spoonful. When you've added half the sugar, pour in the lemon juice.

To assemble the house

15. Join an end wall and a side wall with some icing as shown. (Always hold every section you join for a few minutes before adding another section).

16. Ice the remaining walls into place, and wait about 15 minutes for the icing to dry.

17. Ice the uppermost edges of one side of the house and stick one of the roof panels in place. Make sure that this panel is stuck firm before you add the other one.

18. Ice the chimney together as shown. Leave it to dry and ice it onto the roof.

19. To finish, decorate your house with lots of sweets and sugary icicles piped on with a piping bag.

German History

Germany has seen many changes throughout its turbulent history. Here are just a few key moments in time.

EARLY GERMANY

The *Neandertal*, a valley near Düsseldorf, became famous in 1856, when ancient remains were found there. Neanderthal man lived in prehistoric times. Later, warlike Germanic tribes roamed the land that we now call Germany. These people made tough opponents for the Romans who stretched their empire across this territory 2,000 years ago. The Romans used the natural boundaries of the rivers Rhine and Danube as the limits of their empire.

HOLY ROMAN EMPIRE

After the collapse of Roman power, the Franks ruled the other Germanic peoples. In AD 800, their king, Charlemagne (Karl der Große), joined the tribes together in a great empire that included France and parts of Italy. This was the Holy Roman Empire, and it lasted for a thousand years.

PLAGUE

In the 14th century, bubonic plague swept through Europe, killing a quarter of the German population.

MARTIN LUTHER

A German monk called Martin Luther *(below left)* brought conflict to the Holy Roman Empire during the 16th century by attacking the Roman Catholic Church. His movement became known as the Reformation and those who supported him were known as Protestants. Rivalry between Catholic and Protestant states led to the Thirty Years' War.

THE HABSBURG DYNASTY

In the 15th century, the Habsburg dynasty came to power and stayed there for almost 400 years. During this time, the German principalities split up more and more until there were about 350 separate states.

OTTO VON BISMARCK

In 1806, as a result of the French Revolution and the Napoleonic Wars, the Holy Roman Empire came to an end. Sixty five years later, the prime minister of Prussia, Prince Otto von Bismarck, helped to create a unified Germany. Bismarck was the first chancellor of the new German Empire. The first emperor (*Kaiser*) was Wilhelm I, the Prussian king.

WORLD WARS

The third Kaiser, Wilhelm II, led Germany into World War I. Following its defeat, Germany became a republic, known as the Weimar Republic. The Weimar Republic ended in 1933 when the Nazi party came to power. Their *Führer* (leader), Adolf Hitler, became Chancellor. His aim was to make Germany all powerful, and this led to World War II in 1939. By the end of the war, in 1945, Germany lay in ruins.

A DIVIDED GERMANY

After World War II, Germany was divided into four zones. The capital city of Berlin was situated in the zone occupied by the Soviet Union. The city itself was divided into four parts. In 1949, the Russian zone became a separate state, the German Democratic Republic, while the other three zones became the Federal Republic of Germany. In 1961, the Berlin Wall was erected to divide east and west. This was pulled down in 1989, and many East Germans were able to cross the border for the first time in 28 years. On 3 October 1990, the two German states were officially reunited as one country.

TIME BAND

AD 962 Otto I is crowned Emperor of the Roman Empire
1517 Beginning of the Reformation
1618-1648 Thirty Years' War
1871 Formation of the German Empire
1914-1918 World War I
1919 Treaty of Versailles; Weimar Republic formed
1933 End of Weimar Republic; Hitler appointed Chancellor
1939-1945 World War II
1949 Foundation of Federal Republic of Germany (West) and the German Democratic Republic (East)
1961 Berlin Wall erected
1989 Berlin Wall pulled down
1990 Reunification of the two Germanys

Say it in German
die Geschichte - history
der Krieg - war
der König - king
die Kirche - church

Picture Pairs

Play Picture Pairs and see how many of the German words in this book you actually remember! The instructions given here are for two to four players, but as your German vocabulary increases, you might like to make more cards and include more players.

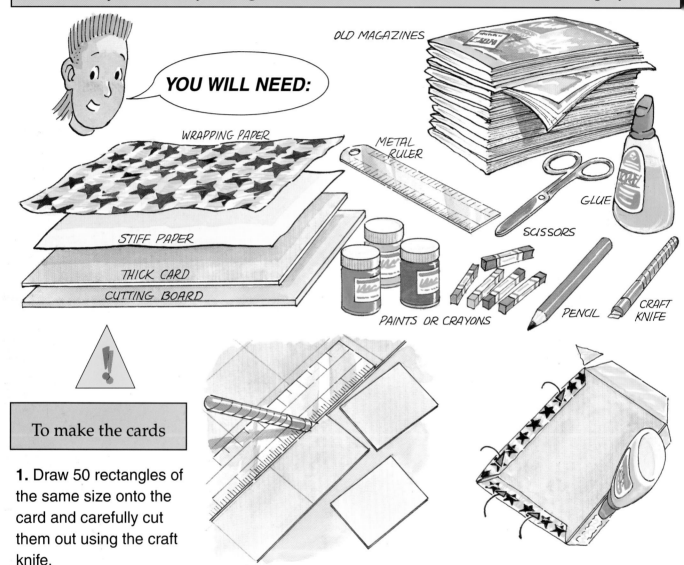

YOU WILL NEED:

OLD MAGAZINES

WRAPPING PAPER

METAL RULER

GLUE

SCISSORS

STIFF PAPER

THICK CARD

CUTTING BOARD

PAINTS OR CRAYONS

PENCIL

CRAFT KNIFE

To make the cards

1. Draw 50 rectangles of the same size onto the card and carefully cut them out using the craft knife.

2. Draw another 50 rectangles onto the wrapping paper and cut them out too. These rectangles should be about 2 cm longer and wider than the card ones.

3. Cut the the corners of the paper rectangles as shown and glue them onto your cards.

4. Draw 25 rectangles, slightly smaller than your cards, onto the stiff paper and cut them out.

5. Choose 25 German words from this book and write them down with their English translations. (Keep this list beside you when you play the game.)

6. Look through the magazines and cut out any photographs which illustrate the words you have chosen. If you can't find suitable pictures, cut out some more rectangles from stiff paper and paint pictures of your words on them.

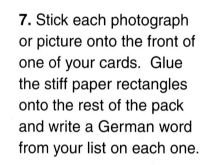

7. Stick each photograph or picture onto the front of one of your cards. Glue the stiff paper rectangles onto the rest of the pack and write a German word from your list on each one.

To play the game
The object of Picture Pairs is to collect pairs of cards made up of words and their matching picture.

Each player starts the game with seven cards. The rest of the pack is placed face down on the table. If you have any pairs, put them on the table in front of you.

Then ask one of the other players if he/she has a card that you need to make a pair. If that player has the card requested, he/she must hand it over and you win the pair and have another turn. If he/she does not have the card, you take a card from the pack in the middle and the turn passes to the next person.

All word cards must be translated into English. If you can not remember the translation of a word, look it up and miss your next go.

The player who pairs all his/her cards first is the winner.

31

Index